CONNECTING SELF WITH SUPER SELF

ATUFA FAROOQ

ISBN 979-888521597-8

Contents

Contents

“And keep reminding, because reminding benefits the believers”

(Quran – 51:55)

Preface

The book contains excerpts and passages collected from many hadith books and the holy Quran itself. It also contains the enlightening and inspirational thoughts and feelings of the author herself. It will be of equal interest to all Muslims whether they are young or old; staunch believers or laymen. The book will benefit everyone. It is a small effort by this budding writer and she wants to bring the people of her generation and others out of the depths of depression, despair, darkness and confusions and wishes to put them on the path of light, happiness, progress and prosperity. The book will serve as a ray of hope for those who grope and fumble in vain in the darkness spread by various modern diabolical institutions. The following couplet sums up the purpose of this book:

Return, return, return to your Lord
Whether you are sinner, disbeliever or hopeless.
The door of the lord is open for everyone.

About The Author

Atufa Farooq lives at district Pulwama in the UT of Jammu and Kashmir. She is the youngest daughter of Farooq Ahmad sheikh and Mehjabin Khan. She is the student of Law. There are few things that she chooses passionately are: Her Iman, health, knowledge. She is an obedient daughter, loyal friend, staunch believer in Islam, writer, calligrapher and more. This is her first book as she wants to make everyone aware about what she has learnt. According to her, the real Islam is beneficial to humankind, whereas some features of cultural Islam may actually contradict aspects of Islam. She adds that, we pray: Allah guides Muslims back to the real Islam which upholds truth, justice, fairness, equality, rights, freedom and so much more.

You can reach her by her email: atufajabeen90@gmail.com

CHAPTER ONE

Allah's Mercy

I don't care how many times you have turned back to Allah and then gone back to your sin, go back to him again because he is the all merciful ,the all forgiving .I know it's hard ,I know that shaytan is making you doubt Allah's mercy but let me tell you something, something that is going to give you hope . Allah swt's mercy overrides his anger, think about it, the one who created you why would not he forgive you? He loves you more than your parents , He loves you more than your loved ones , He knows you more than you do , He knows you more than your best friend , He knows you more than anyone, He hears ,He sees ,He knows you can literally sit in silence and He knows everything that's going on , He knows more than you do of yourself , you can sit and cry and he understands every teardrop ; have sabr.

CHAPTER TWO

Stress is a part of being Human

The Quran clearly tells us that feeling anxious, worried, stressful is a part of being human, there is nothing wrong with that's. Societal problems can and will cause us stress.

Allah says to the Prophet (pbuh):" we know that your heart is in pain, because of what they say."

[Quran15:97]- think about that.

And the next verse then continues to declare the perfection by praising your master, focus your attention not on problems, but on the greatness of Allah.

I am learning something amazing about difficult situations that we may find ourselves in:

"Oh, your heart became or your chest became tight?

You became uncomfortable? Let me tell you what will alleviate your chest or what will bring you peace and tranquility in your heart.

Allah says," so exalt (Allah) with praise of your Lord and be of those who prostrate (to him) [Quran- 15:98]

"And worship your Lord until them comes to you the certainty (that is death)

[Quran-15:99]

I would never replace Allah with my parents to be the judge on the day of judgment, I would rather have Allah judge me rather than my parents on the day of judgment, because Allah knows me more than my parents,

- if you believe Allah loves you more than your parents, Allah will love you more than your parents , If you believe Allah can forgive all your sins, Allah will forgive all your sins , if you believe Allah will reward you and enter you into Jannah , Allah will not betray you your faith in him , Allah will surely answer your dua and enter you into Jannah.

CHAPTER THREE

You are doing wrong and expecting things to be right?

Yousuf (a.s)'s own brother got jealous of him and left him in a deep dark well when he was an innocent child. He was sold as a slave and went through many hardships after that. Years later when he met his brother, he forgave him and blamed shaytan for misguiding them. He didn't taunt them for anything.

This is pure forgiveness and you say you have forgiven but you don't forget to rub salt in their wound?

you feel kick seeing someone embarrassed for their wrongdoings?

- Younus (a.s) repented and made dua to Allah when he was inside the stomach of a whale. He did not blame anyone but himself and he did not question why that was happening to him. He just repented and made dua to his Lord. This is Tawakkul.
- And you bring Tawakkul on soothsayers, talesman and all, then hope your problems to get solved?

- Yaqub(a.s) lost his most beloved son. He cried to the extent that he lost his eyesight. He accepted the Qadr of Allah without questioning anything.

This is beautiful sabr and you make dua today and tomorrow you ask why your dua's have not answered yet?

Don't question Allah's decree but question yourself, why are you being so impatient? -

- Ibrahim (a.s)'s father was an idol worshipper. He tried his best to give dawah to his father but he never raised his voice against him.

This is obedience to parents

And you act as if you have done enough for your parents, you don't care if they live or die?

- when Lut (a.s) asked people to marry with the opposite gender and repent from homosexuality, they said him to go away if he had problem with it , they made him feel that they were all right and he was the abnormal one

Don't think a wrong can be right just because everyone is doing it. So do not ever blindly follow the crowd, follow the truth

- Nuh(a.s) gave dawah for centuries to people yet only a small group of people believed in him and you get angry if someone opposes you in a mere opinion ? You call them kaafir? You get desperate if you get less likes?
- Ibraham(a.s) sacrificed his son for the sake of Allah, he went to slaughter his only son for Allah's pleasure.
- And Allah gave you money, wealth and luxury but you still hesitant to give them on his way (charity)?
- Ayyub (a.s) lost his wealth, his children, his health and his everything, yet he never responded to the whispers of shaytan and never for a second, he forgets to show his

gratitude to Allah.

- And you have everything still you are ungrateful? You watch movies, and seriels but you don't have time to thank your Rabb and say Alhamdulillah?

CHAPTER FOUR

Wearing high heels is Haram?

It's not permissible to wear high heels outside home where non-mahram can see you, there are reasons why scholars may say that high heel shoes are not permissible to wear in public.

• The noise they make attract attention

Allah (s.w.t) says:" let them not stamp their feet to make known what they conceal of their adornment."

[Quran: 24:31]

• Prophet Muhammad (s.a.w) said :" there are two types of people of hell that I have not seen yet : men with whips like the tails of cattle, with which they strike the people, and women who are clothed yet naked, *walking with an enticing gait,* with something on their heads that looks like the humps of the camels , leaning to one side . They will never enter paradise or even smell its fragrance.

[Sahih Muslim 2128]

• They are harmful to the feet, ankles and back. Prophet Mohammad (s.a.w) said:" do not cause harm or return harm."

[Sunan Ibn maja 2340]

CHAPTER FIVE

Four ideas to get you through hardships

1. But perhaps you hate a thing and it's good for you and perhaps you love a thing and it's bad for you. And Allah knows, while you know not. [Quran 2:216]
2. Do the people think that they will be left to say, we believe and they will not be tired? [Quran 29:2]
3. Allah does not charge a soul except {with that within} its capacity [Quran 2:286]
4. Indeed, Allah will not change the condition of people until they change what is in themselves [Quran 13:11]

Take your broken heart to Allah, he is the one who made it and he's the one who can mend it. May Allah heal the broken hearts. The ones who are silent, who cannot express their pain, the ones who are tired of torment, the ones who need a break. May Allah put an end to your sadness, may He put a smile on your face.

CHAPTER SIX

Dangers of disobeying parents.

MAJOR SIN.

- Anas Ibn Malik reported the prophet, peace and blessings be upon him, said regarding the major sins: are associating idols with Allah, disobedience to parents, killing a person and false testimony.

  [Sahih Al- Bukhari 5632]

- Allah's anger

Abdullah Ibn Amar reported The Messenger of Allah, peace and blessings be upon him, said, the pleasure of the Almighty is in the pleasure of the parents, and the displeasure of the Almighty is in the displeasure of the parents [Sunan Al- Tirmidhi 1899]

- Will not enter paradise. The Messenger (pbuh) of Allah said: there are three will who will not enter paradise: the one who disobeys his parents, the drunkard and the one who reminds people of what he has given them.

[Sunan an nasa'i 2562]

• One of the most important acts of worship that the child is asked to do with regard to his parents is to obey them, to do as they ask and to refrain from what they tell him not to do. So if his father tells him to do something, he hastens to do what he is told, and if he tells him not to do something, he hastens to give it up, so as long as that does not involve any disobedience towards Allah and his Messenger, because there is no obedience to any created being if it involves disobedience towards the creator .

Allah says in Quran:

"And we have enjoined on man to be dutiful and kind to his parents" [Quran 46:15]

"But behave with them in the world kindly"

[Quran 31:15]

CHAPTER SEVEN

What a beautiful Deen we have been blessed with:

Rasulullah (s.a.w) said,

No fatigue, nor disease, nor sorrow, nor sadness, nor hurt, nor distress befalls a Muslim, even if it were the prick of, he receives from a thorn, but that Allah expiates some of his sins for that.

[Sahih Bukhari]

• The Prophet (s.a.w) said:

"whoever sits in a place where he does not remember Allah, he will suffer loss and incur displeasure of Allah; and whoever lies down (to sleep) in a place where he does not remember Allah, he will suffer sorrow an incur displeasure of Allah"

[Abu Dawud 4856]

CHAPTER EIGHT

Are you depressed?

• Allah says,

And whoever turns away from my remembrance, Indeed, he will have a depressed life

[Quran 20:124]

• So, turn to Allah because;

Verily in the Remembrance of Allah, do hearts find peace.

[Quran 13:28]

CHAPTER NINE

Eight best advices for your daily life:

1. Do not leave Ayatul kursi after praying five times. The distance between heaven and us is only death.
2. Send more salawat to the Prophet (pbuh) on Friday.
3. Read ten times Surah Al- ikhlas every day. Allah will build a magnificent palace for us in heaven.
4. Pray fajr every day. Allah will ease affairs and increase sustenance.
5. Read and love The Quran.
6. Read Surah Al- Mulk every night before going to bed. The Surah is a barrier from the torment of the grave.
7. Never leave prayer even though our sins are many.
8. If you are lazy to do the sunnah, at least don't leave the sunnah prayer at dawn before fajr. Its reward is greater than the world and everything in it.

CHAPTER TEN

Top four unbreakable promises from Almighty Allah in Quran.

"So, Remember Me, and I will remember you" [Quran 2:152]

- "If you are grateful, I will surely increase you (in favor) [Quran 14:7]
- " Call upon me, I will respond to you" [Quran 40:70]
- " Allah (s.w.t) will not punish them, while they seek forgiveness" [Quran 8:33]

CHAPTER ELEVEN

Seven ways to stop overthinking.

1. Ask Allah: Allah listens, turn each anxiety, each fear and concern into a Dua. Allah knows what is in your heart yet he still listens.
2. Remember that human responsibility is limited

- While we need to carry out our duty to the best of our abilities, always remember that you do not control the outcome of events. Even the Prophets could not control the outcome of their efforts. Some were successful, others were not. Regardless of what your results, you will be rewarded

3.Leave the world behind you five times a day.

- use the five daily prayers as a means to become more hereafter oriented and less attached to this temporary world. Start distancing yourself as soon as you hear Adhan. When you stand in front of Allah, mentally prepare yourself to leave this world and all of its worries and stresses behind you.

4. Seek help through Sabr "Seek help through Sabr and Salat." [Quran 2:45]

• This instruction from Allah provides us with two critical tools that can ease our suffering and pain. Sabr is not just patience, it includes self-control, perseverance and a focused struggle. Sabr includes a duty to remain steadfast to achieve our goals despite all odds. It gives us control in situations where we feel we have little or no control.

1. Allah controls life and death.

- if you fear for your safety and security, remember that Allah alone gives life and take sit back, that he has appointed a time for it. No one can harm you except if Allah wills. As Allah says in the Quran:

"Wherever you are, death will find you, even if you are in the towers built up strong and high." [Quran 4:78]

2. Rely on Allah.

- "When you have taken a decision, put your trust in Allah."
- Once you have established a plan you intend to follow through on to deal with the specific issue on your life then put your trust in the wisest and the All- knowing.

7. Sleep the way Prophet (pbuh) slept.

- End your day on a positive note. Thank Allah for all the good accomplished. Ask yourself what did you do today to help others. Recite Surah Al-Mulk. Sleep on your right side with your hand below your cheek (the way Prophet (s.a.w) used to sleep). End the day with the name of Allah on your tongue, Insha'Allah you will have a good, restful night.

- When someone asks you for help, even just at Dua, make sure to do it. You don't know how desperate they are and perhaps Allah made you a means for them. Tomorrow you could be in their place. Life is unpredictable. And the reward for good is nothing but
- good.

CHAPTER TWELVE

Backbiting?

Many, and by many, I mean a lot of people fall prey to this sin. It is one of the many sins that society has normalized and even encouraged (in songs, movies, TV, realities etc.)

It is only by the mercy of Allah that one can stop indulging in this. We must remind ourselves that it is a major sin, so it's not to be taken lightly. It could lead us to the punishment of the grave and in her hereafter.

It could also be the reason that we lose all our good deeds on the day of judgment.

Giving them all to our victims. And if one has no bad deeds, he could end up burdened by the bad deeds of the one he backbitten about.

"O you who believed, avoid much (negative) assumption. Indeed, some assumption is sin and do not spy or backbite each other. Would one of you like to eat the flesh of his brother when dead? You would detest it.

And fear Allah; indeed, Allah is accepting of repentance and merciful."

[Quran 49:12]

CHAPTER THIRTEEN

How to stop it then?

Repent. Ask Allah to protect you from this sin. Ask him to help you control your tongue and to protect you from shaytaan.

"It's you we worship and you we ask for help" [Quran 1:5]

• when you feel tempted to say something mean, remember that this is the way to lose your good deeds. Don't be the one who spreads the flaws and wrongdoing of others.

"whoever covers (the sins of) a Muslim, Allah will cover him (his sins) in this world and in the hereafter"

[Sunan ibn majah]

• Make Dua , ask him to guide those who seem to be doing bad deeds and to help you see the good in them.

• If you are surrounded by gossiper a backbiter (be it in person or on the social media) politely leave. Staying there might influence you to add one thing or two.

• State it clearly to the people around you: You don't want to be involved in gossip or backbiting.

•Mind your own business, do not spy or try to know what someone is up to just for the sake of knowing. The less you know, the better focus is on yourself.

•Fear Allah. Know that he keeps a record of every single one of your words and action, good and bad.

CHAPTER FOURTEEN

Istikhara prayer?

“Istikhara” means to seek goodness from Allah, meaning when one intends to do an important task, they do istikhara before the task.

- The one who does is asking Allah the Knower of unseen, the guide him /her to know whether the task is better for him / her or not.
- The Istikhara was taught by the Prophet peace be upon him.
- Narrated Jabir bin' Abdullah: The prophet peace be upon him used to teach us the way of doing Istikhara in all matters as he taught us the Surats of the Quran. He said. “If anyone of you thinks of doing any job or marriage or anything important in his life he should offer two rakat prayer other than the compulsory ones and say (after the prayer):
- اللَّهُمَّ إِنِّي أَسْتَخِيرُكَ بِعِلْمِكَ، وَأَسْتَقْدِرُكَ بِقُدْرَتِكَ، وَأَسْأَلُكَ مِنْ فَضْلِكَ الْعَظِيمِ، فَإِنَّكَ تَقْدِرُ وَلَا أَقْدِرُ، وَتَعْلَمُ، وَلَا أَعْلَمُ، وَأَنْتَ عَلَّامُ الْغُيُوبِ، اللَّهُمَّ إِنْ كُنْتَ تَعْلَمُ أَنَّ هَذَا الْأَمْرَ- خَيْرٌ لِي فِي دِينِي وَمَعَاشِي وَعَاقِبَةِ أَمْرِي- عَاجِلِهِ وَآجِلِهِ- فَاقْدُرْهُ لِي وَيَسِّرْهُ لِي ثُمَّ بَارِكْ لِي فِيهِ، وَإِنْ كُنْتَ تَعْلَمُ أَنَّ هَذَا الْأَمْرَ شَرٌّ لِي فِي دِينِي وَمَعَاشِي وَعَاقِبَةِ أَمْرِي- عَاجِلِهِ وَآجِلِهِ- فَاصْرِفْهُ عَنِّي وَاصْرِفْنِي عَنْهُ وَاقْدُرْ لِيَ الْخَيْرَ حَيْثُ كَانَ ثُمَّ أَرْضِنِي بِهِ

- Allaahumma 'innee 'astakheeruka bi'ilmika, wa 'astaqdiruka biqudratika, wa 'as'aluka min fadhtikal-'Adheemi, fa'innaka taqdiru wa laa 'aqdiru, wa ta'lamu, wa laa 'a'lamu, wa 'Anta 'Allaamul-Ghuyoobi, Allaahumma 'in kunta ta'lamu 'anna haathal-'amra-[then mention the thing to be decided] Khayrun lee fee deenee wa ma'aashee wa 'aaqibati 'amree – [or say] 'Aajilihi wa 'aajilihi – Faqdurhu lee wa yassirhu lee thumma baarik lee feehi, wa 'in kunta ta'lamu 'anna haathal-'amra sharrun lee fee deenee wa ma'aashee wa 'aaqibati 'amree – [or say] 'Aajilihi wa 'aajilihi – Fasrifhu 'annee wasrifnee 'anhu waqdur liyal-khayra haythu kaana thumma 'ardhinee bihi
- O Allah, I seek the counsel of Your Knowledge, and I seek the help of Your Omnipotence, and I beseech You for Your Magnificent Grace. Surely, You are Capable and I am not. You know and I know not, and You are the Knower of the unseen. O Allah, if You know that this matter [then mention the thing to be decided] is good for me in my religion and in my life and for my welfare in the life to come, - [or say: in this life and the afterlife] – then ordain it for me and make it easy for me, then bless me in it. And if You know that this matter is bad for me in my religion and in my life and for my welfare in the life to come, - [or say: in this life and the afterlife] – then distance it from me, and distance me from it, and ordain for me what is good wherever it may be, and help me to be content with it. Whoever seeks the counsel of the Creator will not regret it and whoever seeks the advice of the believers will feel confident about his decisions. Allah said in the Qur'an: "And consult them in the affair. Then when you have taken a decision, put your trust in Allah."

- [Al-Bukhari 7:162].
- what needs to be noted is that the answer of ones istikhara prayer does not come simply in the form of dreams and feelings but in how Allah facilitates and unfolds events for an individual after he or she genuinely strives to do what is best.
- Place your trust in Allah.
- One needs to be patient in terms of receiving the answer to their prayers. Remember the words of our Prophet peace and blessings be upon him," the supplication of everyone is granted as long as he does not show haste and does not say that he made a supplication but it was not accepted." [Abu Dawood, Ibn majah]
- And Allah knows best, He is the All-seeing, All-hearing, the best Planner. May he guide us and ease all our difficulties.

CHAPTER FIFTEEN

Best times for dua

1. Between the Adhann and the Iqamah: Allah's Messenger peace and blessings be upon him said," the suppplication made between the Adhan and Iqamah is not rejected."

   [Tirmidhi 212 (sahih)]
   [Abu Dawud 521(sahih)]

2. In Sujood: Allah's Messenger peace and blessings be upon him said," the nearest a servant comes to his Lord is when he is prostrating himself , so make supplication(in this state)

   [Sahih Muslim 482]

3. In the last third of the night Allah's Messenger peace and blessings be upon him said:" Our Almighty, the blessed, the superior comes every night down on the nearest heaven to us when the last third of the night remains, saying: "is there anyone to invoke me, so that I may respond to invocation? Is there anyone to ask me, so that I may grant him request? Is there anyone seeking my forgiveness, so that I may forgive him?"

[Bukhari 1145]

4. The Dua of an oppressed person: Allah's Messenger peace and blessings be upon him said:" Beware of the supplication of the oppressed, for there is no barrier between him and Allah"

[. Bukhari 2448]

5. Dua of a Father and dua of the one traveling:

Allah's Messenger peace and blessings be upon him said:" there are three supplications that will undoubtedly be answered: the supplication of one who has been wronged; the suppplication of the traveler; and the supplication of a father for his child."

[Ibn majah 3862]

Also "the supplication of a father against his son"

[Tirmidhi 1905]

6. Dua when it's raining:

Allah's Messenger peace and blessings be upon him said:" there are two which will not be rejected: Dua at the time of the call (to prayer) and when it's raining.

[Abu Dawood 2540 (sahih)]

7. When the call for the prescribed prayers is given and when the ranks are drawn up for battlethe:

Allah's Messenger peace and blessings be upon him said: "there are two that will not be rejected , or will really be rejected : dua at the time of the call for prayer and at the time of battle when the fighting begins".

[Abu Dawood 2540 -sahih]

8. Dua at a certain time on Friday:

Allah's Messenger peace and blessings be upon him said:" There is an hour (opportune time) on Friday and if a Muslim gets it while praying and asks something from Allah then Allah will definitely meet his demand." And He (the prophet pbuh) pointed out the shortness of that time with his hands."

[Bukhari935]

* that opportune time is the last hour of asr*

9. When drinking zam zam water:

Allah's Messenger peace and blessings be upon him said:" the water of zamzam is for whatever it is drunk for"

[Ibn majah 3062]

10 . Dua made for one who is sick or dying:

Allah's Messenger peace and blessings be upon him said:" when you visit on who is sick or dying, say good things for the Angels say: Aameen to whatever you say"

[Ibn Majah 1447 – sahih]

11. Dua of a righteous person for his parents:

Allah's messenger peace be upon him said:" when the son of Adam dies all his good deeds come to an end except three: ongoing charity, a righteous son who will pray for him, or beneficial knowledge."

[Muslim 1631]

12. Dua at a certain time of night: Allah's Messenger peace and blessings be upon him said:" during the night there is a time when the Muslim does not ask for the good of this world and the hereafter but it will be given to him and that happens every night"

[Sahih Muslim 757]

13. After saying the Dua of Prophet yunus(a.s) : Allah's Messenger peace and blessings be upon him said the supplication of prophet Yunus when he supplicatedhim , while in the belly of the whale was

'there is none worthy of worship except you glory to you indeed I have been of the transgressors'

لَآ إِلٰهَ إِلَّآ أَنْتَ سُبْحَانَكَ إِنِّيْ كُنْتُ مِنَ الظَّالِمِيْنَ

(La ilaha illa anta subhanaka inneekuntu minaz zälimìn)

. So indeed, no Muslim man supplicates with it for anything, ever, except Allah responds to him"

[Tirmidhi 3505 – sahih]

14. Dua made for others:

Allah's Messenger peace and blessings be upon him said:"The supplication of a Muslim for his brother at his back(in his absence) is responded so long as he makes supplication for blessings for his brother and commissioned Angel says: Ameen, and says : May it be for you too"

[Sahih Muslim 2732, 2733]

15. Dua when sun has reached its zenith: Allah's Messenger Peace and blessings be upon him said: "This is the time when the gates of heaven are opened and I want a good deed of mine to ascend during this time."

[Tirmidhi 478-sahih]

16. Dua when hearing the crowing of a Rooster:

Allah's Messenger Peace and blessings be upon him said: "when you hear the crowing of a Rooster, ask a lot of his bounty, for he has seen an Angel"

[Muslim 2729]

17. Dua when calamity befalls a Muslim: Allah's Messenger Peace and blessings be upon him said:" There

is no calamity that befalls on some of the Muslims and he responds by saying:" Indeed we belong to Allah and we will have to return to him. O Allah, recompense me for my affliction and replace it for me with something better.

But Allah will compensate him with something better than it.

[Sahih Muslim 918b]

CHAPTER SIXTEEN

Just a reminder

Sometimes what you asked for was not good enough for you but you think you know best. Allah will take it away from you and you still think you know best but Allah never gives up on you, and soon the day comes when you receive what Allah has planned for you and you realize how much better it is. You wonder what even made you want anything else in the first place.

Allah knows best.

Alhamdulillah, Allah knows your true worth, He saves you from things that are never going to be good enough for you , even when you are not grateful for His plan yet, this is how much He loves you , He will not let you settle for less than what He has planned for you and when you realize it and see the truth , your heart , mind and words will say Alhamdulillah a million times.

CHAPTER SEVENTEEN

Tips to focus better in Salah:

1. Allah stays right in front of you.

• Remind yourself time to time, that Allah (s.w.t) is right in front of you, when you're praying Salah.

2. Be keen to pray perfectly.

• Know that you may not get the entire reward of praying Salah unless you pray it correctly. So take your time when you pray, instead of rushing, so that your sole focus is on completing the Salah correctly and not on million other things .

3. Meaning of the recitations.

• Try to reflect upon the meanings of the adhkar of the prayer and the verses of Quran that you would recite in your Salah , because this is one of the greatest means of attaining presence of mind and not letting one's heart be distracted.

4. Environment.

• Try to pray in an environment where there is less/ no noise. There should not be anything in the place that may distract you, such as image and sounds etc. especially prohibited sounds such as singing and music. This will make it easier to focus on your Salah rather than what's going on around you

5. Allah is seeing and hearing.

• Remind yourself that you're praying to Allah and not just reciting alone. Allah is always listening and he knows what is in your heart while you perform Salah.

6. Sometime before Salah

•Just 5 or 10 minutes before you perform your Salah, keep your phone, laptop, and everything aside. Sit alone for a while and do dhikr. Say Alhamdulillah for all the things you have. It will help your mind to think less about the duniya, when you start your Salah.

7. Remember about death

• Keep in your mind that this could be your last Salah. Think that in your last Salah you would want to stay focused and pray properly.

If you want to know what attachments take you away from Allah, then look at what you often think of when you're in Salah

CHAPTER EIGHTEEN

What can you do for those who are dead?

. Making dua for them.

. Istagfar for them.

. Sadaqah jariah (on going charity) on their behalf. [Sahih Al- Bukhari 2756]

. Fulfilling the oaths that they made in their life. [Sahih Al-Bukhari 7315]

Hajj and umrah on their behalf [Sahih Muslim 1149].

CHAPTER NINETEEN

Love your parents and spend your maximum time with your parents:

- Our parents are often misunderstood.
- When mom comes and sits in your room, she isn't invading your personal space. Sometimes she's just trying to escape her own thoughts.

• "Don't use the Sharpness of your speech on the mother who taught you how to speak "[Ali Ibn Talib]

- Every time your mother asks you, "what are you smiling at"? when you're using you phone, she isn't being nosy , she just wants to be a part of your life , because the two of you barely talk anymore.
- Every time your father asks "where are you"? It feels like an investigation, but he just wants to know
- You know, mom doesn't hate ' eating from restaurant ' she hated that she has cooked food for you, but you ordered instead and when she cooks your favorite food, all she hopes to hear you say is," It's tasty"

- I know, I know there's a generation gap, but let's not forget, while we are growing up, they are growing older too. They are humans, too. And just like us, our parents can feel lonely and are misunderstood.

- I guess, all that we can do is listen to them.

Thus, God has enjoined on us to show kindness, respect, and humility to our parents. We are commanded to do this, even though they may have injured us. The only exception to the above command is made in the following verse:

"We have enjoined on man kindness to his parents; but if they strive (to force) thee to join with Me anything of which thou hast no knowledge, obey them not."

(The Quran 29:8)

CHAPTER TWENTY

How can a person avoid sins when alone?

• The Muslim in this world is vulnerable to falling into sin and disobedience. What is required of him – if he does fall into sin – is to hasten to repent and seek forgiveness.

- "And whoever does a wrong or wrongs himself but then seeks forgiveness of Allah will find Allah forgiving and Merciful" [4: 110]

1. Turning to Allah.

. And when my servants ask you, [O Muhammad], concerning me – Indeed I am near. I respond to the invocation of the supplicant when he calls upon me. So, let them respond to me [by obedience] and believe in me that they may be [rightly] guided. [2:186]

2. Striving to control the nafs (self, and its evil inclinations)

. And [by] the soul and he who proportioned it, and inspired it [with discernment of] it's wickedness and its righteousness, he has succeeded who purifiers it, and he has failed who instills it [with corruption] (91: 7-10)

. "And those who strive for us – we will surely guide them to our ways. And indeed, Allah is with the doers of good [29: 69]

3. Bearing in mind that Allah is always watching.

. If you're ever alone, do not say I'm alone; rather say I've one who is watching me. Don't think that Allah is ever unaware even for a moment, or that anything is hidden from him.

4. Remembering death and imagining if death were to come to him whilst he was committing that sin; how would he meet his Almighty in that case?

"Remembering what Allah has prepared for his righteous slaves of Paradise as vast as the heavens and the earth, and thinking of the punishment of Allah, may he be exalted.

Indeed, those who inject deviation into our verses are not concealed from us. So, is he who is cast into the fire better or he who comes secure on the day of resurrection?

Do whatever you will; indeed, he is seeing of what you do. [41: 40]

5. Conceal the sin from people

They conceal (their evil intentions and deeds) from the people, but they cannot conceal (them) from Allah, and he is with them (in his knowledge) when they spend the night in such as he doesn't accept of speech. And ever is Allah, of what they do, encompassing. [4:108]

*May Allah protect me and you from sins and acts of disobedience, and help us to restrain our lower selves (nafs and evil inclinations)

CHAPTER TWENTY-ONE

Are you silently suffering?

Tell Allah what's wrong. Tell Allah why you're sad. Tell Allah why your heart feels heavy. Tell Allah why you feel like you're sinking. Tell Allah why it hurts. In ways you can't even explain. Tell him because he cares. Tell him because he brought you this far and only, He can take you even further. And if you need help, who can help you other than Allah? Talk to Al- Wali (The Protecting friend), cry to Al – Wadood (The Loving God). He will heal you. He will help you. I promise.

*Sometimes all you can really do is Converse with your Almighty about everything. It's the only way that anything will ever change. You can talk to your friends for as long as you want. You can go to your family about it all too. But they're not the ones who can really help you. They listen, sure. They care, of course. Allah is the only one who knows what's inside your heart. You can't keep secrets from Allah. He's there to help you, protect you, grant you good, take away the bad, guide you, forgive you, shower you with his mercy, love you and to keep you happy. So, don't forget him, because he tells us,

"Remember me and I will remember you"

[Quran 2:152]

CHAPTER TWENTY-TWO

The answer to your Supplications is Delayed for a reason

There is an interesting situation that confuses many: the believer who is afflicted with the calamity and then invokes Allah constantly, yet sees no signs of an answer to his prayers then when he comes near to the point of hopelessness, the true worth of his heart is found out. If he is pleased with what Allah decreed for him, without losing hope of Allah's Favor, then in most situations it is at this point that such a person's supplications are answered, because his test is over: his faith has shined through and the Devil has been defeated. So, it is at the time of near hopelessness that the worth of man is judged. This meaning is alluded to in the saying of Allah:

"Or think you that you will enter paradise without such (trials) as came to those who passed away before you?

They were afflicted with severe poverty and ailments and were so shaken that even the Messenger and those who believed along with him said," When (will come) the help of a law yes certainly the Help of Allah? "Yes! Certainly, the Help of Allah is near!"

[Quran: 2:124]

After Ya'qub(a.s) lost his son, much time elapsed yet he never lost hope of relief instead of relief , another of his sons was then taken away, and even then he did not lose hope of a lost favor and mercy :

"So, patience is most fitting (for me). It may be that Allah will bring them all (back) to me. Truly He! Only He is All-Knowing, All-wise."

[Quran 12:83]

And similar were the words and sentiments of Zakariyyah(a.s):

"And I have never been umblest in my invocation to You, Oh my Lord!"

[Quran 19:4]

Never, therefore should one feel that too much time has passed by without his applications being answered. One should realize that, whenever one is tested with hardship, one's mettle and faith are being tested. To pass such a test, one must drive away the whispers of the Devil and then turn for help to the Most-Merciful, Most-Generous, the Most-Wise.

"O friends of mine who have acted recklessly against their own selves, do not despair of Allah's mercy. Surely, Allah will forgive all sins. Surely, He is the one who is the most – forgiving, the very merciful.

-Atufa Farooq

9 798885 215978

Printed by Libri Plureos GmbH in Hamburg,
Germany